broccoli nose

frog-foot nose

shriveled nose

stuck-up nose

mushroom nose

jelly roll nose

button nose

This notebook is dedicated to Elisa Kleven
because she writes and draws way cooool!
(and she's great with scissors)

Hey, you! mouth

sour lemon mouth

silly mouth

rubberband mouth

you don't need to copy—you can make
your own notebook—right here!

Marker conforms to ASTM D4236
requirements. Manufactured in
Malaysia.

way, way,
far away!

luscious lashes eyes

mean monster eyes

squinty eyes

letter i's

bug eyes

hair in your notebook

springy hair

polka dot clown hair

Mohawk hair

hair in your soup

Martian ears

An AMELIA Book

pierced ears with earrings— yay!

bunny ears

←this is not a butterfly split apart—it's ears

3 cheers for Tricycle
Hip! Hip! Hooray!

TRICYCLE PRESS
P.O. Box 7123
Berkeley, California 94707
Book Design by Amelia ←yahoo!

ear muffins

ear-resistable!

Uh-oh—these numbers remind me, I forgot to do my math homework

freshness date— use this notebook by

First Tricycle Press Printing, 1997
Manufactured in Singapore

4 5 6 — 00 99 98

OK, it's all yours. A brand new **BLANK** **ANYTHING** notebook. You can do in it!

You can use
or
or
or

(only the paper might get soggy and wrinkly, so watch out)

← stickers

→ rubber stamps

or even invisible ink.

Whatever **YOU** want. No one's the boss of your notebook, but you. (Now you know why I love to make notebooks!)

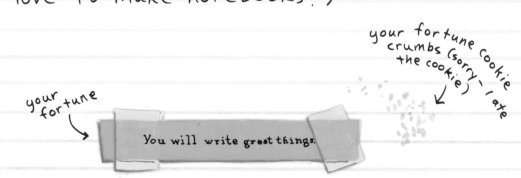

your fortune →

You will write great things.

your fortune cookie crumbs (sorry - I ate the cookie) ↓

If your name isn't __Dana__   ← you again!

KEEP OUT!

If you look in here you will fin' out!

The Evil Eye will find __Dana__ wherever they go — even in the bathroom.

someone you definitely do not want to see your notebook

← The Evil Eye will find

Evil Eye

Evil Eye

Hey! I want privacy!

flussh!

8

Do not look in
here ~~[scribbled out]~~ Robbie and
Byan

Things that make me feel good:

the smell of cinnamon

comic books, especially when read in bed with a flashlight

hot chocolate

your favorite song on the radio

clothes warm and toasty from the dryer

a fresh clean pillowcase on your pillow

finding lucky money

if you find money, then it's lucky

puurrrrr

petting a cat— it's impossible to stay mad or sad when a cat purrs at you

being in charge of the remote

brand-new markers

pumpkin pie

filling in all the squares on a crossword puzzle

stars on a clear, clear night

making a wish on a star on a clear, clear night

BOO!

Halloween

a cool breeze on a hot day

birthday parties

mmmmm

the last piece of cake (especially when Cleo wants it, too)

do skates go this way or this

ice-skating— but not falling down

PESTUS ANNOYUS
10¢
mosquitoes

dull scissors that mangle your paper

shoes with sand in them

There you are, snookie!
relatives who pinch your cheeks

Yuuch!
driving home from the beach in a wet bathing suit so your tush sticks to the seat

SPLAAT!
toast falling butter-side-down

potato masher thingy that lives in the kitchen drawer and, for some mysterious reason, never gets used

little melon scoop that gets used once a year when Great-Aunt Edna visits 'cause she's the one who gave it to Mom in the first place

This is your notebook, so you get to do <u>whatever</u> you want. Me, here's what I do— sometimes I write stories, sometimes I write whatever I'm thinking (well, worrying) about. Writing is ~~weird~~ ~~wierd~~ ~~weird~~ ~~wierd~~ weird. It's kind of like cooking because you throw a bunch of stuff together, and you never know how it will all turn out (at least, that's how <u>my</u> mom cooks).

spelling is even worse— weirder— weirder— I give up!

Help— there's a tablespoon on my mind.

— uh-oh— the secret's out!

Amelia's Secret Family Recipes for Writing

Recipe for a Journal
1) Take 3 tablespoons of what's on your mind.
2) Stir well and chew it over.
3) Season with descriptions — spice it up!
4) Gobble it up! Don't let <u>anyone</u> else see it.

Recipe for a Story
1) Take 1 cup Something Interesting.
2) Mix in an exciting beginning.
3) Add 3 teaspoons characters (I mean, who is this story happening to, anyway?)
4) Blend with a dash of plot (what happens next?)
5) Simmer until well done.
6) Serve piping hot (yum!) How does it taste?

strange fancy vinegar that Mom bought when she decided to become a great cook (only she never did)

Bulls-eye!

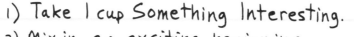

Cleo putting raisins up her nose and snorting them out — veeeery interesting!

add salt

dig in!

Cutlery
Cuties

12¢

FAMOUS
FOODS

11¢

↑
eggzactly!

H
A
N
G
I
N
G

HOT
DOGS

3¢

2   3

food
for
thought
↓

FOOD
FESTIVAL

80Z 4N4

pepper anyone?

it's

good

to

eat

it!

tallest sandwich in the world

tallest mouth
to eat it

Once upon a fish

I also LOVE to draw pictures and make up stories about them. I just start to draw, and whatever I draw starts to talk. I draw some more, things talk some more — a story happens!

It's a cow that jumped over the moon— not a pig!

We'll see.

But I wanted chocolate on top— maybe I should lick from the bottom up.

We could make a beautiful fruit salad together.

That's my time I will see ice cream

shell with eyes glued on to make a creature

souvenir ball you shake and snow comes down

Interesting Things to write about:

big saps

pen with picture that moves when you shake it

your temperature is going up!

goofy eyeball cap

stick-on earrings

mood ring—stone changes color with your mood

sea monkies

knitted kleenex-box cover

piece of wood with a postcard decoupaged on

little viewer with pictures that change when you click the button

Yeah! Go for it!

WRITE ON!

← freshly sharpened

↑ no teeth marks

clean and pink

SAMPLE FIRST SENTENCES:

"I couldn't wait to write about it in my notebook."

"I got out my markers and started to draw."

"It was all Cleo's fault."
(It always is!)

"He started it!"

"She shook the package and tried to guess what was in it."

Well If I did do my homework
Wath will hope to me!
I hare no doe be I mit
fnde out!

Surprise!

But The Dire sll: gas
no!

"Once upon a time, I had to go to the bathroom."

elitzpje!

"It was a dark and stormy night."

"The dog burped."

Excuse me!

"First he put on one shoe, then the other."

Too big!

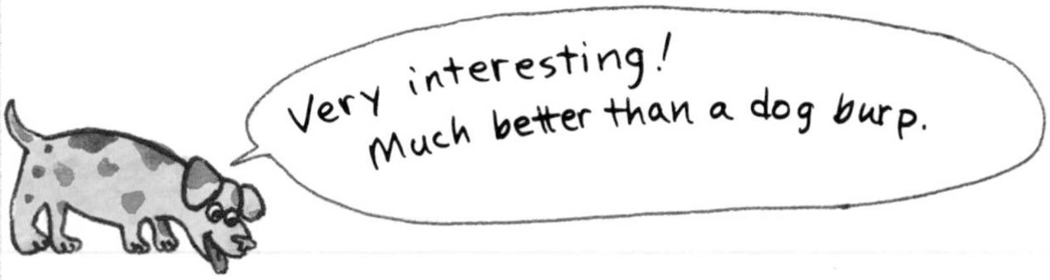
Very interesting! Much better than a dog burp.

CHARACTERS

I have known — and some I've made up.

comfy bunny slippers

Jumphigh-runfast shoes

spiffy gotta-dance shoes

cowboy boots with fringe—yeehaw!

When I imagine a character and write about them, it's kind of like wearing someone else's shoes.

penny loafers with pennies

somebody's-got-to-wear-them shoes (but not me!)

ballet slippers

thongs, zorries, flip-flops, beach shoes, or just plain rubber thingies

clip-clop clogs →

frog feet

rubber boots that pull your shoes off with them when you take them off

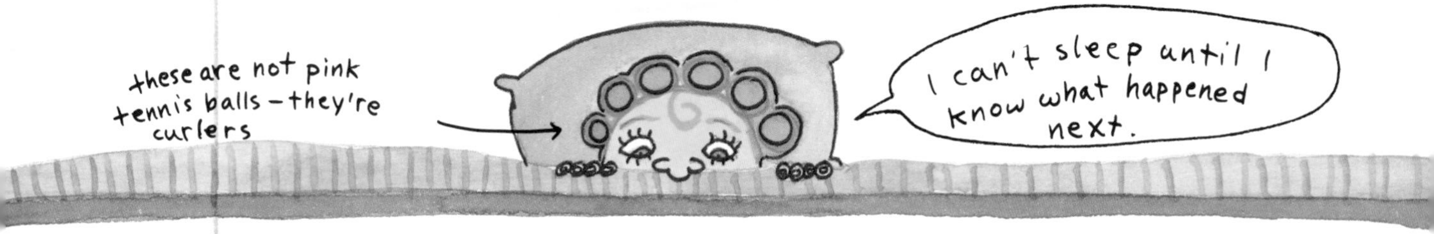
these are not pink tennis balls – they're curlers
I can't sleep until I know what happened next.

I love you!

First ending:

Dog wags tail.

Sometimes I try ending a story four different ways.

Second ending:

Tail wags dog.

Third ending:

Tail and dog wag together.

Fourth ending:

Hot dog wags at tail and dog.

← Mustard

← ketchup

← relish

Do you think there are too many hot dogs in this notebook?

I f go#t up to her Sop.

Bird eats apple-
yum!

Second ending:

Bleh!

Bird hates apple-
there's a worm
in it—yuuch!

Third
ending:

Bird is stupid-
thinks apple
is an egg and
tries to hatch
it!

Fourth ending:

Mama

Apple is an egg!
It hatches!

I can't wait to get out the flashlight and read this in bed.

It must be a grown-up saying this.

Turn out that light!

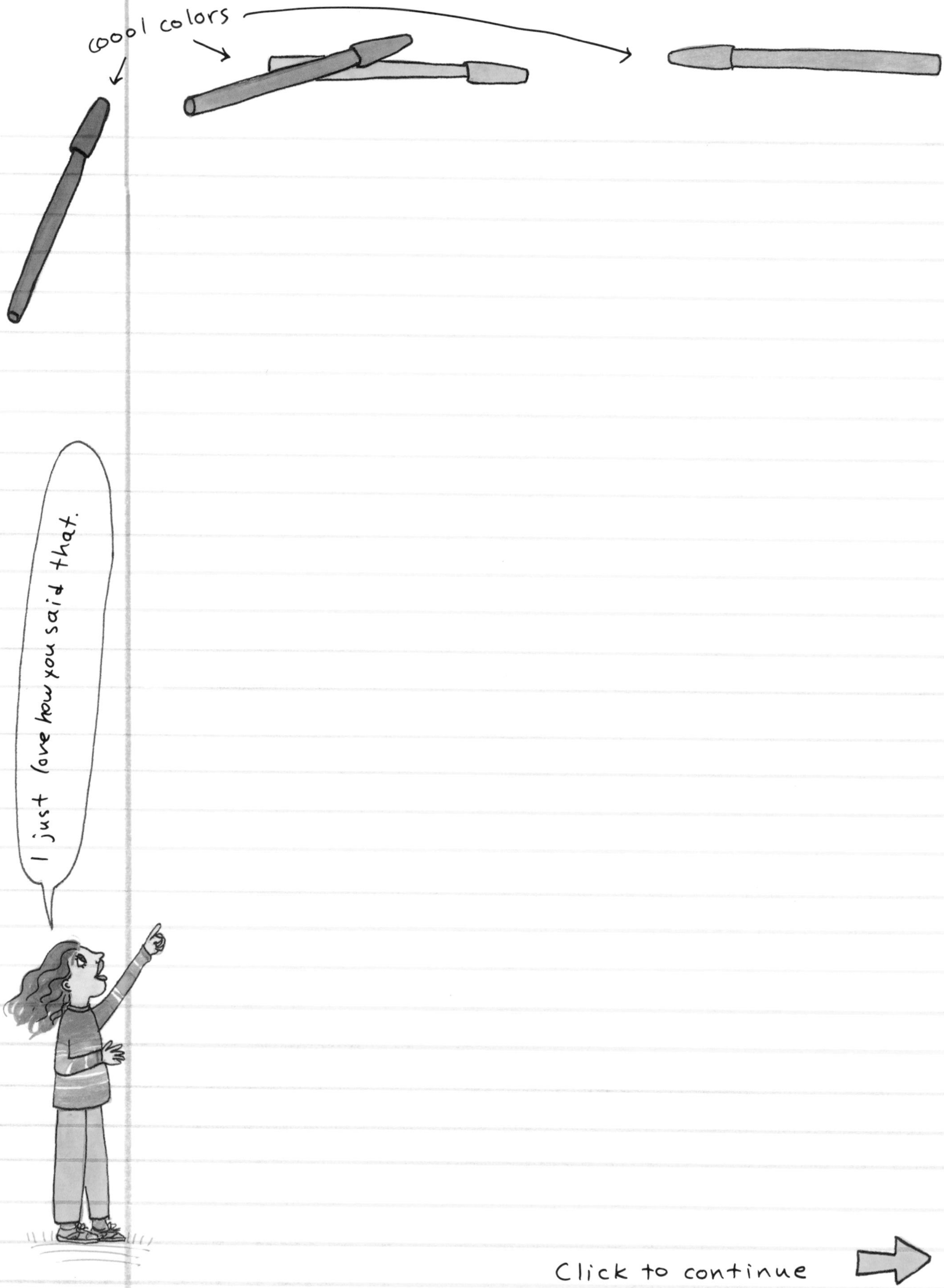

Click to continue

Hairdo Page

ice cream
hairdo

umbrella hairdo

pizza
hairdo

witchy hairdo

donut hairdo

Statue of
Liberty
hairdo

idea lightbulb goes on

Super idea!

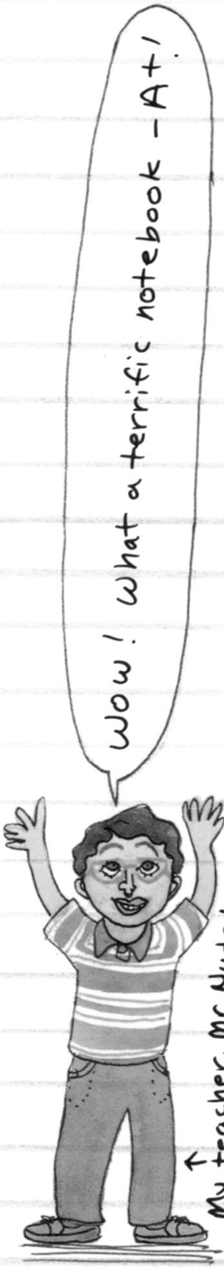
WOW! What a terrific notebook - A+!
My teacher, Mr. Nudel

GROSS FOOD PAGE

liver—
the smell
alone is
poisonous

Never eat anything
with bumps, lumps,
or little green
things in it!

green beans—
scientists are
still searching
for proof that
these are edible

stinky, gooey
cheese—the kind
only grown-ups
eat and when
they do, it's
disgusting to be
around them
because they
stink just like
the cheese

meatballs
and meat loaf—
no mystery
meat for me!

scrambled eggs
with runny white
part— the only thing
worse is a soft-boiled
egg — yuccch!

tofu—
I don't eat
squishy square
foods — uh-uh!

caviar—
I say it's
fish eggs
and just because
it's expensive
doesn't mean
it tastes good

fish—anything
that smells that
bad, can't taste good

This isn't a mess – it's confetti to celebrate your notebook.

Tell me more (it's not secret, is it?).

Sometimes, when I'm too tired to write a whole story (or letter), I just write a postcard.

14¢
Cupo' Reglar

HA HA HA
COMIC MUSEUM

Dear Nadia,
I'm having fun writing in _another_ notebook.
I just can't stop writing! (And drawing, too, of course.) What kind of things do you have in _your_ notebook?
    love, your friend forever,
        Amelia I M TRU 2 U
(P.S. If it's secret, you don't have to tell me.)

Cup o' Joe 18¢

Nadia Kurz
61 South St.
Barton, CA
91010

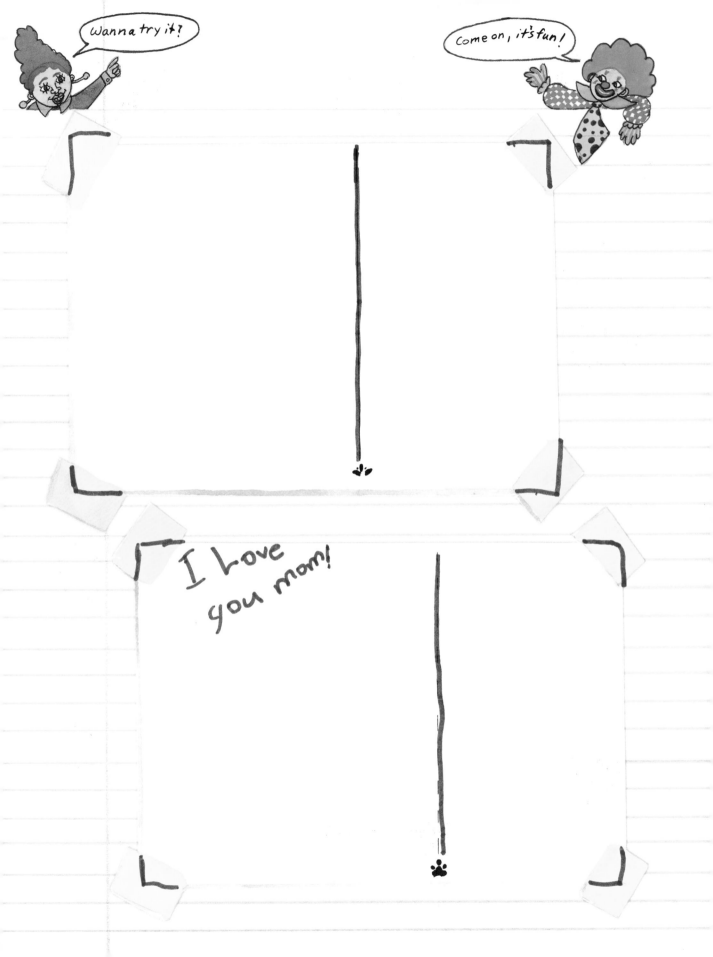

I don't always need a postcard — I can find a whole story in a tiny stamp.

Poetry Page!
Rhyme Time ← hey, that rhymes!

flow

crow

row

grow

pro

whoa

yo-yo

blow

dough

mow

low

owe

bough

woe

slow

Joe Schmoe
wore a bow.
He tripped on a hoe
and stubbed his big toe.
It started to snow.
Joe's car wouldn't go.
He shouted, "Oh, no!
I'll be late for the show!"

↑
this poem
is so-so

blow   throw   stow   tow   sew   glow   foe

wax dripping on cheap-o wine bottle

lightning, thunder, and rain

Bloop! Bloop!

plug-in lava lamp from a garage sale

Some things remind me of a bunch of other things. Like I can't smell a new car without remembering how I threw up in Grandpa's new Oldsmobile. (He kept plastic on the back seat for a year after that.) That's kind of like poetry. (Not the throw-up or the plastic, but the way your mind goes from one thing to the other, from new-car smell to throw-up smell.)

moonlight

sunshine

the smell of fresh-cut grass

creaking stairs

shadows

footsteps

nose sniffing a funny smell

birds singing

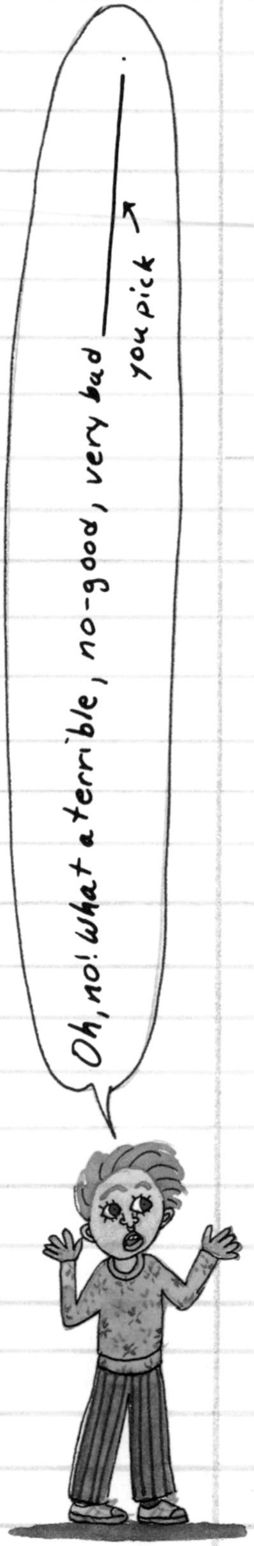

Oh, no! What a terrible, no-good, very bad ______ .
you pick

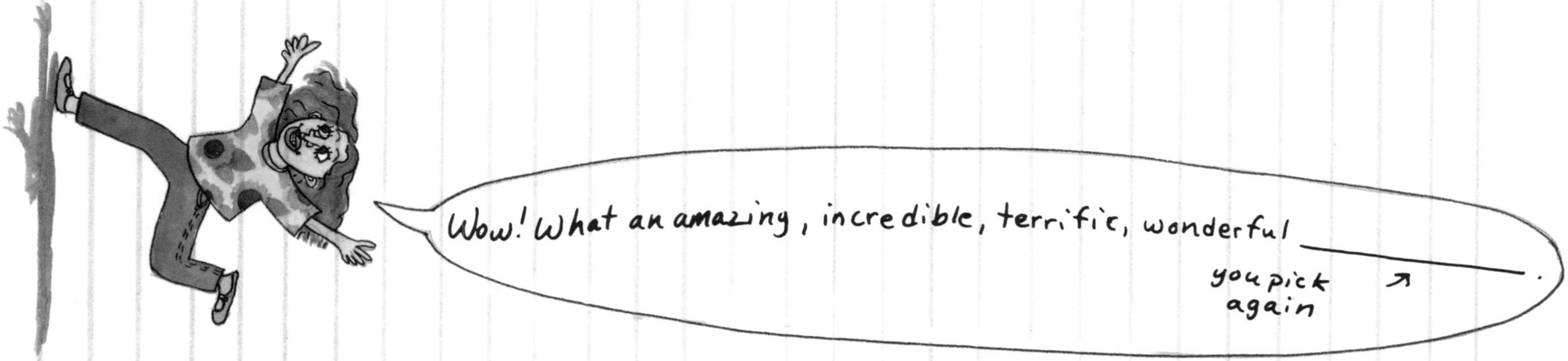
Wow! What an amazing, incredible, terrific, wonderful ______.
you pick again

dark
closet

worry doll → under the
under the
pillow

under the
bed

Dreams are like stories your brain makes up for
you (and sometimes I haaaate them).

scary face
in the wood
grain of a
door

shadows

← I had a nightmare that a ghost came in my bedroom
window, but when I woke up, it was just a tree clawing
at the glass.

branch scraping against the window

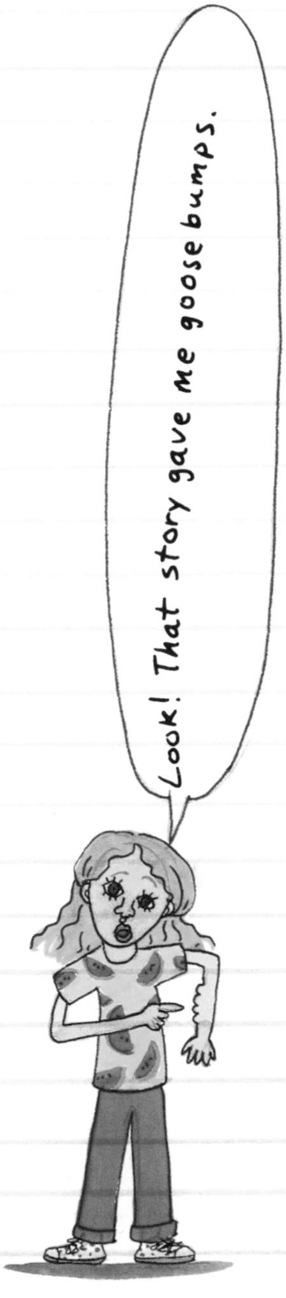
Look! That story gave me goose bumps.

First prize for a great
notebook — it's all yours! →

The secret to making this ribbon look so cool is that I didn't
make a pen outline, just a light pencil one. Pretty good, eh? →

fortune
cookie
fortune

You will make many more notebooks.

good luck for you!

a good
sharp pencil

W is for
Wonderful
Work

a fresh pink eraser

GOOD WORK
SEAL OF APPROVAL

a cool
marker